MINDSET

How you can become powerful and achieve success on your terms

By: Patricia A Carlisle

Introduction

I want to thank you and congratulate you for choosing the book, *"**MINDSET: How you can become powerful and achieve success on your terms**"*.

This book contains proven steps and strategies on how to achieve success on your terms.

People believe their basic qualities, like their intelligence or talent, are simply fixed traits. They spend their time documenting their intelligence or talent instead of developing them. They also believe that talent alone creates success- without effort. They're wrong.

Being successful and feeling successful are quite different things. Reaching other people's version of success does not come with the joy and happiness that you were hoping for. Success is a word that means many different things. Chasing someone else dreams means betraying your own dreams, and should be something you should try to avoid. This book will help you to define your version of success, and show you how to get it done on your terms.

Thanks again for choosing this book, I hope you enjoy it!

ABOUT THE AUTHOR

Patricia A. Carlisle, MSW, CBT

Patricia Carlisle- a Master Social Worker and a Cognitive Behavioral Therapist (CBT) gives out an expression of how important it is for an individual to take into consideration the concept of self-assessment to know what human, technical and conceptual skills they posses to perform or to achieve what they desire, or to deal with everyday life. However, every particular group of people has their own unique set of ideas, traditions and events including the frame of mind according to which people perform but there are many who faces problems and fail to maintain a healthy mind set affecting their behaviors and performance to those around them.

People like Patricia Carlisle are among those who have felt this urge of serving people and helping them out of their mental crisis towards a healthy life. She has experienced some close encounters in her personal life regarding mental health issues in her family and friends that has encouraged her to pursue this as her career.

Currently Patricia Carlisle is serving as a Certified On-Line Cognitive Behavioral Therapist with an extensive 15years of experience using Cognitive-Behavior Therapy Techniques. She envisions a world where everyone gets mental health treatment with no mental health stigma and to make it real she has already set up her own Holistic Measure Online Comprehensive Behavioral Healthcare Company after retiring from The Nord Center in The Partial Hospitalization Program (PHP) Dept for 5 years and Murtis H. Taylor Mental Health Center as a mental health counselor, psychological support technician and case manager for 10 years to emulsify her skills more professionally. Along with this, she has wrote down her passion as a clinician in 25 or more short books to help individuals and families get their life back, freeing them of the restraints of negative thinking, anxiety and depression by using different approaches. She is highly appreciated among her clients for her flexibility and professionalism of dealing with them graciously. To reach her, make use of her direct website address: http://therapist2013.wix.com/e-therapy . As she is ready to inspire hope and contribute to health and well-being by providing the best online health care through comprehensive practice, education and research.

TABLE OF CONTENT

MINDSET

How you can become powerful and achieve success on your terms

Chapter 1

WHAT IS MINDSET

Chapter 2

POWERFUL STRATEGIES TO HELP YOU ACHIEVE ANY GOAL

Chapter 3

HEALTH AND WELLNESS

Chapter 4

WAYS TO DEFINE AND ACHIEVE SUCCESS ON YOUR TERMS

Chapter 5

RULES FOR SUCCEEDING IN YOUR OWN BUSINESS

Chapter 6

THINGS YOU SHOULD GIVE UP TO BE SUCCESSFUL

Conclusion

Preview Of 'MINDFULNESS EXERCISES FOR BEGINNERS'

Chapter 1

WHAT IS MINDSET

Mindset is a simple idea discovered by a decade of research on achievement and success—a simple idea that makes all the difference.

In a fixed mindset, people believe their basic qualities, like their intelligence or talent, are simply fixed traits. They spend their time documenting their intelligence or talent instead of developing them. They also believe that talent alone creates success-without effort. They're wrong.

In a growth mindset, people believe that their most basic abilities can be developed through dedication and hard work-brains and talent are just the starting point. This view creates a love of learning, and a resilience that is essential for great accomplishment. Virtually all great people have had these qualities.

Teaching a growth mindset creates motivation and productivity in the world of business, education, and sports. It enhances relationships

Chapter 2

POWERFUL STRATEGIES TO HELP YOU ACHIEVE ANY GOAL

1. **Innovate:** Instead of waiting for change to find you, continuously innovate on your job to stay ahead of it. Take the initiative to come up with ideas for doing things better-and then have the courage to advance and implement them. Thinking differently is looking at everything and figures out where and how you can contribute, and then do so.

2. **Collaborate:** One of the best ways to advance your career is to think, "How can I help others succeed?" When your team wins, you win along with it. It's not all about you-when you're a team player, you build a strong foundation for your own success. Who gets credit is irrelevant. What matters is that as a team you are doing great work, achieving your goals. Steer people in the right direction. Make others look good-your clients and colleagues, bosses, and employees. Be a true team player, and success will come back to you tenfold.

3. **Google it:** With Google at your fingertips, you no longer have to tell your boss "I don't know" when you're asked a question you don't know the answer to. Instead, you can say, "I will find out," and have an answer quickly and easily. Today, we have an opportunity most people didn't, to surf our way to become an expert, or at least dangerously close-with Google as a secret weapon.

4. **Rethink dedication:** When a boss gives you an assignment, as a dedicated employee you usually jump right in-sometimes without thinking. Instead of racing to a solution, step back for a moment and think about how you can do it better and smarter. Go beyond normal dedication to think about alternatives. Apply logic to your work. Do more than is asked of you. There is always a better, faster way to do things. Work smarter-not-harder-and you will outwit your competitors, and move up in your company at a rapid pace.

5. **Chase Skills, not titles:** We all want to get promoted in our jobs, and achieve the job title that go along with those promotions. This is a mistake. People get so focused on what they should do that they lose sight of what they could do. Your success in the long run won't come from working for a dream company, or holding prestigious job title. It depends on the skills and abilities you learn and bring to the table. Think of your career in terms of building blocks, each block representing a set of skills-and then do the work. Do whatever it take to acquire the skills that will help take you to the next level. This takes guts, and a willingness to turn a traditional career path on its head.

6. **Practice persistence:** What's the one common attribute high achievers share above anything else? PERSISTENCE. When they have a goal, they simply refuse to give up until they reach it-no matter what roadblocks life throws in their way.

   Consider the stories of the individual who attempted to reach the North Pole seven times before he finally succeeded, can you believe number eight. Or the screenwriter who wrote the screenplay for Dallas buyers Club in 1992, and struggled for 20 years to get his script turned into a movie-which became a huge success and won numerous awards, including the Oscar for best original screenplay. You can read about them and many other ordinary people who have persevered to achieve extraordinary success in The Success Principles. I encourage you to read about these people so you can learn from their examples and be inspired by their stories. It's a great way to reignite your own motivation!

7. **Face what isn't working:** If you are going to become more successful, you have to get out of denial and face what isn't working in your life. Are your goals simply too big to accomplish in the time you have available? Are you lacking some essential skills required to achieve them? Are you in denial about the amount of support you need?

   Successful people face these circumstances squarely, heed the warning signs, and take appropriate action, no matter how uncomfortable or challenging it might be.

   Do you need to talk to someone? Ask someone for help? Find a new resource? Read a book? Call an expert? Make a plan to fix it?

Choose one action you can take and then do it. Then keep taking another action and another action until you get the situation resolved.

8. **Transcend your limiting beliefs:** Sometimes the biggest reason we don't move forward is because deep down we don't think we're actually capable of achieving our goals-or deserving of the success we long for.

   If you have limiting beliefs or negative thoughts holding you back from reaching your goals, take some time to identify what these thoughts and beliefs are, and then transform them into an empowering belief using these four steps:

   - Write down the negative belief.

   - Describe how the belief limits you.

   - Decide how you would rather be, act, or feel.

   - Create a turnaround statement that affirms your right to be, act, or feel this new way.

9. **Stay motivated with the masters:** Motivation comes from within-but sometimes you need an external nudge to push you forward in the right direction.

   Whether you're commuting by car or train, riding your bike, going for a run, or simply find yourself with a few minutes in front of the computer, listening to audio or video recordings can give you the edge you need to excel in virtually any area of your life. You can keep yourself motivated, learn a language, learn management skills, learn sales and marketing strategies, learn better communication, and learn about holistic health and more. By devoting more time to developing success-oriented thoughts and attitudes, you are guaranteed to reach your goals faster.

10. **Take BOLD actions to get BIG results:** When you start a new project take on a new venture, or put yourself out there, there is usually some fear. Unfortunately, most people let fear stop them from taking the necessary steps to achieve their dreams.

Successful people, on the other hand, feel the fear along with the rest of us, but don't let it keep them from doing anything they want to do-or have to do. They understand that fear is something to be acknowledge, experienced, and taken along for the ride. And they challenge themselves to take bold action, trusting that they have what it takes to handle the outcome.

Think big-and act bigger. By taking a leap of faith in the face of fear, you can transform you life.

Remember-you cannot copy success. But you can design it.

Chapter 3

HEALTH AND WELLNESS

- **Clearly define what it is that you want to do:**
  Very successful people care about their lives more than
  the average person. They take the time to analyze their
  lives, to look closely at their vision and their purpose in
  life. They put their lives on paper. They take the time
  to construct mental images that guide them on their
  journey. While most people are winging it, they put
  their life mission and business vision and goals on
  paper. They have imagination. They pull their
  imagination up in their mind, and then they define
  their vision and then they go to work. Night and Day!

- **Protect and Manage your Time:** Successful
  Entrepreneurs Protect and Manage their time. How
  many people do you know that plan their day before it
  begins? The most valuable asset you have is your time.
  Plan your days, weeks, months, and years.

- **Outcome Oriented:** Have you know anyone that is
  absolutely driven to succeed? No matter what the
  obstacle they keep going. And in most cases it is
  because they have extraordinary clarity on the
  outcome. They took the time to clearly define what it is

that they wanted to do. They stopped and thought about their life, and what it was that they wanted to accomplish, and this gave them the drive to see the task all the way to its outcome.

- **Deal with Actual Facts:** Most people make their decisions about their life and careers from emotion and assumptions. Successful entrepreneurs base their decisions from fact-based thinking. Successful entrepreneurs strive to make accurate decisions rooted in Actual Facts.

- **Live To Provide Value:** Successful Entrepreneurs know that value must be given. And by providing value they know that value is to be returned. They practice the Law of Reciprocity. They know for sure what they give out they shall receive. Successful entrepreneurs do not expect something for nothing. They are constantly working to make themselves valuable, which of course attracts the personal associations that lead to greater financial success.

- **Perform a Mind Makeover:** Successful people rarely resemble the person that they once were. They are constantly education themselves, and gaining experience that will lead them to the goals they desire. They truly understand the importance of acquiring greater skill sets, which in turn gives them a confidence boost and greater self-worth. They live by the words of 'renewing their minds'. These entrepreneurs know this is the key to their transformation and growth.

- **Focus:** This characteristic is what I have found to be the most important when it comes to entrepreneurial success. Once you have awakened to the possibilities of success, you also realize the many opportunities that abound. And it is easy to allow yourself to become scattered. Successful people develop the ability to focus and concentrate to maximize their resources and forces.

- **Success by Association:** Did you ever heard when growing up "be careful who you hang around". Many times you may be 'guilty by association'. Well, successful entrepreneurs understand that you can also be 'successful by association.' In fact it is virtually impossible to be successful without having a mentor, or a friend, or business associate that helps to quicken your advancement. Successful entrepreneurs have someone that accelerated their advancement with either some knowledge they possess, or some other resource that they did not have.

- **Understand Self and Others:** When you constantly work on yourself, you begin to develop a greater understanding of yourself, and greater belief in yourself, which translates into valuing yourself. This is what allows you to become an expert in your chosen area. If you don't understand and value yourself then you can bet the entire farm that no one else will understand or value you. Those who understand and value themselves have a greater ability to understand and value others. This skill set is so important when you are seeking higher levels of success.

- **Take Personal Responsibility:** This trait is it. This removes all attempts to blame anyone for what takes place in your life. Successful entrepreneurs never allude to anything that anyone could have done to them. In fact, all the trials that they have, they looked at them as a blessing to learn from. Never giving up control of their lives. All of these keys, traits, and skills sets make up the Mindset of Successful Entrepreneurs. You could probably think of other variations, but somehow you will end up dealing with these principles.

Chapter 4

WAYS TO DEFINE AND ACHIEVE SUCCESS ON YOUR TERMS

It's easy to get caught up in what we think we should be doing in order to invite success into our lives. We read blogs, we subscribe to newsletters, we talk with family members and friends, we peruse Pinterest, and we follow people on Facebook-there's information and advice galore out there. We live in a remarkable time with remarkable tools for learning and for social interaction.

While there are obvious advantages to having access to so much information, it's also a bit of a slippery slope. It's easy to begin believing that other people outside of yourself have all the answers. If you just do what so-and-so-blogger says to do, then you'll be successful. It's easy to compare yourself to other people who create similar types of things, and to wish you had their success. It's easy to believe that everyone has it figured out except for you and that you're doing it all wrong.

The thing is, so-and-so doesn't know you. What worked for these folks might not necessarily work for you. They don't know the details of your life, the things you like to do, what scares you, what your strengths are...but you know who does? Yep, you!

I'm here to give you permission to take your power back and define success on your own terms. You know what you need to do, for you. No one could possible know better than you. Take time to get quiet, listen, and then move deliberately forward-the answers will come. The more you work that inner voice muscle (we've all got one!), the easier it'll be to live into your own version of success.

Here are five powerful ways to start tuning into your own inner voice, and defining what success looks like, according to you:

1. **Create [Your name Here] Land:** Close your eyes and dream up what your ideal life might look like. One where you feel the most like you, where you're filled with joy, where you're doing work that you love, where you're surrounded by the type of people you resonate with. Don't worry if it seems crazy or unattainable. Just sink into that feeling of a life you would love living, and let yourself marinate in it.

   - What do you see/hear/feel/smell/taste/etc?

   - What's the best part of your day?

   - What do you not have to worry about?

   - How do you feel? (Aim for three to five core feelings.)

- Who is with you?

Using this worksheet, write down every keyword and experience that feels important from your dreaming time. Then, circle the ones that intuitively speak to you the most right now. Think about:

- What can you do to bring more of those feelings and experiences into your life right now?

- How can you use these dream discoveries to craft your personal definition of what success is for you?

2. **Unsubscribe From Every Blog and Newsletter That Make You Feel "Less Than," icky, or Overwhelmed:** If it makes you feel icky, it's not for you-simple as that. Nothing that you're taking in should make you feel bad about yourself. Unsubscribe! Even if you think you should read it because everyone else is, or because they're an industry expert, or whatever-if it makes you feel icky or small, get rid of it. Then bask in the feeling of empowerment that follows!

3. **Assess Your Current Beliefs About Success. Question Everything:** Take five minutes to quickly write down all your beliefs about success. Don't think about it too much-just get your initial thought on the page as fast as you can. Look over the list. Really think about each belief you wrote down. Is it something you truly believe? Is it something you picked up from childhood? Are there beliefs that need updating? Cross out all the beliefs you disagree with.

Make a list of new beliefs about success. Take a new mental snapshot of what success looks like to you. If it's helpful, start with this phrase: "I am willing to believe that success is..."Sometimes this phrase is helpful because it can give you some space to move into the belief and try it out. Read this phrase every day, to remind yourself of your new belief.

4. **When I'm Successful, I'll Feel…**Write down five important ways you want to feel successful as person. Maybe you want to feel supported, creative, powerful, innovative, on the cutting edge, calm, joyful-there's no right or wrong here. Only you can know how you ultimately want to feel in your life. Next, for each feeling, think of five ways that you can start creating more of it in your life, and your creative business right now. Consider what would change if you used those feelings as guideposts in your decision-making and strategizing. Doing more things that make you feel the way you want to feel will lead to more success.

5. **Take Three Small Steps Toward Success Every Day:** Adopt the idea of doing three things every day that lead in the direction of your definition of success. Small steps in a deliberate direction can add up quickly and lead to big successes! This is also a way to keep from feeling overwhelmed with all the things that need to be done to move in the direction of your dreams-choosing three things to focus on each day is manageable and is something our brains can easily understand.

    Write down your three steps each morning, or at the end of each workday. And here's the key: do your three steps every day, so you create momentum, and it becomes a habit. You'll be on your way to achieving goals and living your successful life in no time. Last but not least, remember that you are in command here. I invite you to step into your power, to decide what your version of success is, and then start living into it. You already have all the answers that you need inside you. Get quiet, listen, and then move deliberately forward, and you'll be moving toward the life of your dreams.

Chapter 5

RULES FOR SUCCEEDING IN YOUR OWN BUSINESS

What does it take to start and succeed in business? Although there is no one answer that fits all businesses, there are a number of practices followed by successful business owners.

No matter what you sell, you'll be ahead of the game if you live by these ten essential rules for succeeding in your own business.

What does it take to start and succeed in business? That's a question I get asked a lot. Although there is no one answer that fits all businesses, there are a number of practices followed by successful business owners. No matter what you sell, you'll be ahead of the game if you live by these ten essential rules for succeeding in your own business.

1. **Be true to yourself:** No matter how much money someone else makes, if you don't enjoy the business, wouldn't be proud to show your relatives what you are doing and how you are doing it, then don't do it. If you run a business you don't like or don't believe in, even if

you have temporary success, it will come back to haunt you one way or another.

2. **Find a need and fill it:** Yes, you've heard that a million times. But it still works. The easiest business to run is one that produces products or services that people already know they need. The reason: you don't have to spend a lot of time and money convincing prospects they need what you sell. You can focus on why you are the best source to satisfy their need. Just be sure the "need" is something one person will spend money for and be satisfied.

3. **Choose products or services that you can sell for a lot more than it costs you to make or buy them:** If the difference between you cost and selling prices is too low, you will have difficult growing the business. When profit margins are too low, you won't have enough money to hire employees, pay for rent (when you need to move the business out of the house), advertise more, and do other things needed to expand.

4. **Make realistic estimates of your expenses...then double them:** Most new businesses either forget about marketing, fulfillment, overhead costs, income taxes, and self-employment, or greatly underestimate them.

5. **Be true to your customers and prospects:** Don't promise what you can't deliver. Don't lie or exaggerate the benefits of what you sell, and always deliver a quality product or service. Word-of-mouth marketing has always been one of the primary ways small businesses find customers. The internet and social networking sites spread the word (good or bad) to even more potential customers.

6. **Understand the importance of marketing and learn how to do it effectively:** The world won't beat a path to your door just because you build a better mousetrap, or write a great eBook about how to grow tomatoes, or teach a child to read. To get customers you will have to market you products or services effectively and continually.

7. **Treat your vendors, manufacturers, and service providers with respect, and let them know you appreciate them:** They are an important part of your team and your success. If you speak down to them, pester them with questions you could answer yourself, imply that they don't do a good job, nickel and dime them to death, or are an ongoing pain in the neck, they'll never go out of their way to help you-and might drop you all together. No business needs picky, annoying, time-consuming customers.

8. **Embrace the web:** No matter what you sell or to whom, your customers will turn to the web to research and/or buy. They may turn to online yellow pages to find a florist in another city or state; use voice recognition on their smart phone to find a nearby restaurant, or use their computer to go to Google, MSN or Yahoo to search for a phrase, or If customers can't find you in their queries, they are likely to give their business to one of your competitors.

9. **Don't expect miracles:** Yes, people do make money in their sleep, or while they're away on vacation- the internet makes that possible. But only after they've invested a lot of time effort, and money in building the business, and building the team that keeps it going and growing.

10. **Backup your work on your computer:** One product, one service, one main client, and all your records stored on one computer hard drive without regular off-site backups is a recipe for failure. If you

only have one product or service you're missing out on the chance to profit by selling more things to people who already know and trust you. If you have only one main client, you're up the creek if they decide to change vendors, or run into cash flow problems. And if all your records are on your computer, and you don't have always up-to-date backups of your important files, a hard drive crash could destroy your business.

Chapter 6

THINGS YOU SHOULD GIVE UP TO BE SUCCESSFUL

1. **Give Up Your Mask:** In order to avoid getting hurt and rejected, we hide who we really are behind a mask of who we think we should be. Have the courage to be you, to show your true emotions and stand behind them-even at the risk of disapproval. Embrace not only the "good" side of you, but also the vulnerable side.

   Because vulnerability is authentic and real. It's the source of creativity and innovation. It creates opportunity.

2. **Give Up Your Belief In The Future:** Yes, your future holds your hopes, your dreams and desires-but your future depends on the choices you make today. Believe in the presence. You only ever have this moment-because the past moments are gone, and the future will eventually show up as another moment of now. Success starts at this very moment, with the choices you make right now. Practice presence. Notice what's around you, what you see, hear, taste, and smell. Notice what you experience and interact with it.

3. **Give Up Your SOS (Shiny Object Syndrome):** Whether it's chasing that next "shiny" idea, or the secret shortcuts to success-we are all guilty of this addiction. The pursuit of everything that seems appealing is seductive. It makes us go side-tracked, loose focus, and go in a million different directions. Take time to identify the ideas and activities worth pursuing, and then stick to them on a consistent basis.

4. **Give Up Your Need Of Other's Approval:** You sabotage your success if you make choices that aim to avoid disapproval. Your ego's seeking of recognition is never ending and makes you miss potentially rewarding opportunities because of your fear of being criticized. Choose wisely between what's good for the ego, and what's good for your success.

5. **Give up Taking "No" As "No":** Interpret feedback the way you choose to: A "no" doesn't mean "no"-it just means "not right now" or "not this way". Whatever it is that you want to achieve, don't take rejection as a final answer. Take it as a useful feedback that says, "keep going".

6. **Give Up Distinguishing Between Your Private And Work Life:** All aspects of your life are interconnected. You are fooling yourself by believing your private life doesn't impact your entrepreneurial success. You are hindering your growth if some areas of your life are a mess. True success encompasses all areas. Bring passion, perseverance, and joy to all of the roles you play: as an entrepreneur, a lover, or a friend...Make all aspects of your life successful and be proactive.

7. **Give Up Your Reluctance To Ask For Help:** Be man or women enough to admit you don't know everything. Don't take asking for help as a sign of weakness. Instead, embrace it as an act of strength: if indicates honesty, intelligence, and your rise above the ego that wants to do it all alone.

8. **Give Up Fixing Your Weaknesses:** We live in a society that emphasize the need to be well-rounded. Successful people hardly ever mark that box-instead they know, embrace, and manage around their weaknesses. Fixing weaknesses is just another strategy to play safe-playing not to lose instead of playing to win. Change your focus from fixing weaknesses to capitalizing on your strengths-because you will grow the most in your areas of talents.

9. **Give Up Being Perfect:** Perfectionism is based on the false belief that if we do things perfectly, we can avoid failure. It's an unhealthy quest to make your work flawless in order to earn approval and acceptance from others. Recognize the distinct difference between giving your best, and trying to be perfect. Ask yourself if spending the extra time will make an equivalent difference to your success in the long run. Always favor progress over perfection.

10. **Give Up Playing Small:** We are all afraid of failure, so we play small. Playing a bigger game means following your own path. Listening to your intuition, doing what feels right compared to doing what everybody else tells you to do. By playing small, you are not serving yourself or anyone else. Instead play big, go out of your comfort zone. Be prepared to be wrong and fail. Be prepared to feel fear.

11. **Give Up Your Dependency On Willpower:** Regardless of willpower being limited or not-tasks done on autopilot require less thoughts, decision-making and energy. To be successful, you have to act successful.

Align your actions with your goals. Create routines that automate taking the right actions. Be intentional about setting work, health, fitness, and relationship habits. Automate your behavior, one habit at a time.

12. **Gibe Up Your Resistance To What Is:** The present moment is out of your circle of influence. You can't change what is happening right now. Instead of wasting your energy complaining, being upset, annoyed or disappointed, learn to fully accept the present moment and your current thoughts and emotions. What is more insane than resisting something that can't be charged? Acceptance doesn't mean approval. It doesn't mean you can't take action to change an undesirable situation.

13. **Give Up Trying To Be Too Clever:** Be different and innovate, but not for the sake of being different, but out of a quest to make things better. Overcome your reluctance to make use of proven methods and good advice. Don't try to be clever in order to earn other people's approval, and enhance your self-worth. Act out of a desire for improvement and service, and you will end up being clever in the process.

14. **Give Up Waiting For Luck:** Luck builds its foundation on preparation. To be successful, you don't just have to be lucky to come across good opportunities, but you have to be ready and prepared to make use of them. Be the right person in the right place at the right time through preparation. Lucky people act in a way that increases their change of good opportunities. Be open-minded and optimistic. Prepare for your luck then go out and find it.

15. **Give Up Other People's Versions Of Success:** Being successful and feeling successful are quite different things. Reaching other people's version of success does not come with the joy and happiness that you were hoping for. Success is a word that means

many different things. Chasing other people's dreams means betraying your own dreams. Define your version of success and give up all the others.

Conclusion

Thank you again for choosing this book!

I hope this book was able to get you ideas on how to become successful at everything you do.

The next step is to practice the steps outlined in this book to get you started on the road to success.

Finally, if you enjoyed this book, would you be kind enough to leave a review for this book on Amazon? It'd be greatly appreciated!

Thank you and good luck!

Preview Of 'MINDFULNESS EXERCISES FOR BEGINNERS'

Chapter 1: WHAT IS MINDFULNESS?

So what does it mean to be mindful? As a child I was occasionally told, -Mind your manners! This mean I should be aware of what I was doing and how it was affecting other people-usually adults! That's not a bad start; mindfulness certainly is about paying attention. Paying attention to what is happening right now, right before our eyes-and ears and nose and other senses, including our internal ones. Also, what pains and tensions are there in our body, how are you feeling right now, are you aware of what you are thinking or are you on automatic, daydreaming, or perhaps going over and over a difficult encounter? Many of the problems mentioned above relate to the future or the past. Anxiety and stress can result from worrying about future events. Depression is often associated with replaying past events in our mind. We go over past are events or we are anxious about the future.

Mindfulness Exercises For Beginners mindfulness, mindfulness for beginners.

Check Out My Other Books

Below you'll find some of my other popular books that are popular on Amazon and Kindle as well. Alternatively, you can visit my author page on Amazon to see other work done by me. (https://amazon.com/author/patriciacarlisle)

LETTING GO: Learn How to Embrace the Future.

COMMUNICATION SKILLS AND TECHNIQUES FOR DUMMIES.

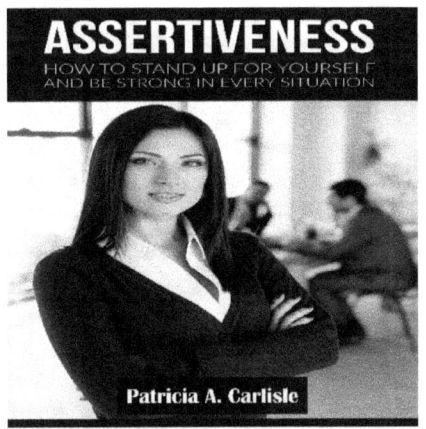

ASSERTIVENESS: How to stand up for yourself and be strong in every situation.

A GUIDANCE TO MENTAL TRAINING: LEARN HOW TO DEVELOP MENTAL RESILIENCE.

MENTAL HEALTH MATTERS: LEARN HOW TO IMPROVE YOUR SHORT-TERM MEMORY.

FAILURE IS NOT AN OPTION: LEARN HOW TO OVERCOME THE FEAR OF FAILING.

THOUGHTS AND FEELINGS: HOW TO BRING YOUR THOUGHTS AND FEELING BACK TO THE PRESENT.

BONUS: SUBSCRIBE TO THE FREE BOOK

Beginners Guide to Yoga & Meditation

"Stressed out? Do You Feel Like The World Is Crashing Down Around You? Want To Take A Vacation That Will Relax Your Mind, Body And Spirit? Well this Easy To Read Step By Step

E-Book Makes It All Possible!"

Instructions on how to join our mailing list, and receive a free copy of "Yoga and Meditation" can be found in any of my Kindle eBooks.

NOTES

NOTES

NOTES

NOTES

www.ingramcontent.com/pod-product-compliance
Lightning Source LLC
Chambersburg PA
CBHW072314200526
45168CB00014B/1472